To: Aley

From: Viki 4|18|18

And we know that in all things God works for the good of those who love him, who have been called according to his purpose. For those God foreknew he also predestined to be conformed to the image of his Son, that he might be the firstborn among many brothers and sisters. And those he predestined, he also called; those he called, he also justified; those he justified, he also glorified.

Romans 8:28-30

GAME CHANGER
A Playbook for Winning at Life

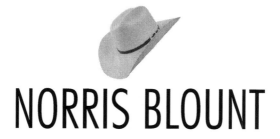

NORRIS BLOUNT

True Potential
REACH THE WORLD

GAME CHANGER
A Playbook for Winning at Life

Norris Blount

Cover and Interior Page design by True Potential, Inc.

ISBN: 978-1-943852-82-6 (paperback)
ISBN: 978-1-943852-83-3 (ebook)
Library of Congress Control Number: 2017962293

True Potential, Inc.
PO Box 904, Travelers Rest, SC 29690
www.truepotentialmedia.com

Printed in the United States of America.

CONTENTS

FOREWORD

Norris Blount and Mel Blount,
4 Super Bowl Championships,
Pro Football Hall of Fame

On August 11, 1966 a boy was born by the name Norris Blount, the son of Mel Blount and Mary Brown. Norris was nurtured by his two grandmothers, Alice Blount and Lucille Brown. Their love for the Lord was evident in all aspects of their lives and was lived out daily. Looking back, I am deeply grateful for the role these two godly women played in Norris's life because his mother and I were just kids when he was born; I was starting college and his mother was trying to figure out what she wanted to do.

While I was in college there wasn't a day that went by that I did not think of Norris. Even though I wasn't with him, I had the peace knowing that he was being deeply cared for because of our strong family unit. He was loved and nurtured in such a way that would lay the foundation that would make him the man he is today. Eventually his mother married and they all moved to Germany where

Norris spent several years before returning to Lubbock, Texas where he would grow up, go to high school and play sports. After high school Norris received a scholarship to Baylor University to play football.

I had the pleasure and honor of going to Norris's games to watch him play. After graduating from Baylor, Norris signed a free agent contract with the Atlanta Falcons. After he was released from the Falcons, he came and worked for me at the Mel Blount Youth Home in Claysville, Pennsylvania. Eventually Norris went to work for corporate America.

Norris is my hero because he has inspired me as a father. He loves the Lord, he knows the word of God and he lives it. I hope this book, *Game Changer*, will help you on your journey as you navigate through life. Norris has shown all of us how to live life and who to believe in.

Norris has shared the gospel all over America and served as the assistant chaplain at Baylor University where we shared the gospel with hundreds of students over the years while in that position. It is amazing how God has used Norris's life not only to spread the gospel but also gave him a vehicle to provide hundreds of jobs for people through his company. I am so proud of Norris. As I said earlier, he is my hero and a leader for our family.

Mel Blount

ACKNOWLEDGMENTS

Reading and writing isn't my passion, speaking to people is. Compiling this playbook took some help from a few people who must love me a great deal because this was not easy. I want to thank my wife Denitia, my dad and my entire family for returning phone calls and filling in blanks I do not remember. This would not be as interesting without the stories of a few of my friends, Brett Garvin, Terri Shankle, Jimmy Shankle, Randy Bruno and Bobby Boynton . I thank them all for contributing time and details that really show what Jesus Christ can do for lives. Lastly, my longtime friend and promoter, Julie Barron who believed anyone would want to read my story and is crazy enough to have me working on the next book already. Thanks be to God for family and friends, AMEN.

INTRODUCTION

God has a plan.

I've been hit in the head many times. Running with the ball in my arm sometimes the last thing I remember is an arm or shoulder hitting my helmet before the thud of the ground. Then lights went out for a second or two. After years of playing football, I sometimes wonder if I've always had to think a bit longer or if a few tackles might have helped. There are days when things are cloudy, and I don't remember names, dates, or what my wife wanted from the grocery store. Serving the Lord, running a business, being a husband, father, son, friend, playing a little tennis and enjoying an occasional nap keeps a man of 50 quite busy. My life is simple and blessed. I go to bed early. I get up early. I walk. I pray. I have fruit. I spend time with my beautiful wife, (I haven't been hit in the head that many times). I pray some more to thank God and study. I plan my day and work begins. It is 6 AM.

Some experts can tell you how to do everything you need or want to do. I am not one. Along the way, it has been pointed out to me, that my life has had some experiences that can help others. A life I did not choose, that has been filled with people who inspired and changed me. People who lead me to dedicate my life to Jesus Christ, and now I want to share these game-changing stories with others.

Very little in my life is different from yours. We have the same hours in a day; we have people to see. We have probably even shared some of the same sadness and joy along the way. If you get nothing else from hearing me speak or reading any of my books know that I am a friend. I want you to know your savior, Jesus Christ, loves you.

This is a playbook. It is designed to speak to those of us who love the game of football and understand the idea that every play counts. This guide can give coaches and players an insight into what it was like to grow up in the footsteps of greatness, my dad Mel Blount. It may help many see the true greatness I see in him as well in the man off the field. This book can be a weekly inspiration to get a team through a season. For a coach, there is a message: as a leader, you are more than someone assigned to win games. You have an opportunity to win lives. My stories are here to help you remember that you are important to the work God needs to be done in the world. There are passages from the Bible that will tie into the message in meaningful ways that can lead to a discussion with others along your path. God's words are timeless, and by His design, apply in situations you will face. Use them to inspire and lead people to become believers in the Lord.

My playbook is about how God will change your game. He changed mine, and I have witnessed him change many others. There are thousands of young lives which may not know Jesus Christ can make them a winner for life.

I am a vessel. God sent one perfect man to teach us how to live and love each other, and we still aren't doing it. One day God let me know He could use me to talk to people about His Book, not mine, and that's what I want to do. I am just an ordinary man that has opportunities every day to tell people about Jesus Christ. One life, God uses every day to read His word and to share His word. I am telling my story, not because I have had a remarkable and amazing life, but because God is using me to share the remarkable and amazing things He has done for us. The journey that has led me here has been God's plan, not mine. Maybe God's plan will change your life or help you change the lives of others. By sharing with people how He is doing the very same in your life right now, maybe, it will change you the way it has changed me. Use me, use my words to help the people you will encounter to have a heart for the Lord. God wants them to win for eternity. Use one chapter, one verse, one experience from my life, or from some of the beautiful people I will share with you, to share with others. God changes everything in a life. Winning is EVERY-THING, as long as we are in the right game.

Norris C. Blount

CHAPTER 1

WE ARE ALL THE SAME, WE ARE ALL IN THE GAME

Our journeys are all the same. From the moment we are born we take our first breath until the final moment in this world when we exhale our last breath, we are the same. God created each of us in His image, and He gave us unique qualities. The world uses the things that make us unique to divide. If you choose to look at people through the eyes of God, you see similarities. If you look at people through the goggles of the world, you will see differences.

> If you choose to look at people through the eyes of God, you see similarities. If you look at people through the goggles of the world, you will see differences.

When you look at me, what do you see? I am just like you.

My skin is black that is my race… Ummmhmmm, and it is AMERICAN BLACK, and I am an American. My parents are Americans, and they are black as well. I am married, I am a father. I am a son, a brother, an uncle, a cousin, a grandson, a boss and a neighbor. My wife is not black, so my children are bi-racial. Isn't this important? We are all Americans at my house and we also all love Cheerios. I typically wear a big Stetson cowboy hat like Walker Texas Ranger. My hairstyle is shiny because I am bald. I love my bald black shiny head. At 6'2", 205 pounds, with my boots and hat, my starched shirt and slacks, people usually think I am the law. I usually let them think that.

> We are all Americans at my house and we also all love Cheerios. I typically wear a big Stetson cowboy hat like Walker Texas Ranger.

I was born in Vidalia, Georgia, and lived with, or spent most of my time with my grandmother, Alice until I was five. My grandmother raised all the grandchildren. I was very close to two cousins near my age. One cousin was the first person to tell me I should be a preacher and the other was my best friend; we played every day for hours. My grandmother made me feel loved, safe and secure. I loved the way she cooked, mmmm hmmm, and I would cry when I had to leave. I am just like you, to feel safe and loved and fed is a wonderful feeling. Do you see that when you see me?

My mom married, and we moved to Germany and then to Lubbock, Texas. Home of Buddy Holly, Mac Davis, Reese Air Force Base, prairie dogs, and me. I love Lubbock, Texas! My mom did shift work at Texas Instruments. She was strict because she knew it was up to her to raise good children. My step-father was a mechanic in the Air Force. When he left the Air Force, he opened a Bar-B-Q restaurant that he still runs today. They both worked hard to give us a comfortable life.

My mother is an extraordinary and beautiful woman. She was just a kid when I was born, and she was determined that she would do everything in her power to raise me the very best she could, and she did.

My mother is an extraordinary and beautiful woman. She was just a kid when I was born, and she was determined that she would do everything in her power to raise me the very best she could, and she did.

She has never accepted excuses. She set the bar high in my life, and she loved unconditionally. My step-father is also an amazing and dependable father. He provided for his family and loved me as his own. He is a man much like Joseph, who was the father of Jesus. We were an average family. I had a younger brother who looked up to me very much and a baby sister. My family was just like most families.

I didn't have many friends at school. I was very shy. My teachers seemed to like me though because I was always at school on time and I was a happy kid. I liked my teachers, but I what I really loved about school was lunchtime! They used to make everything from scratch at school, and I would think, mmmm-mmmm, what is for lunch Toooo DAY!? Chicken fried steak with cream gravy, mashed potatoes in a big scoop, buttered green beans, or maybe peanut butter cookies? I loved lunch time. The fellowship of laughing and being with my friends. I remember being very happy. It might have been the food, but I believe now that God had his hand on me, directing my footsteps even then. Those lunches were delicious. The fellowship was feeding me. Listening to my friends, sharing things going on with their families and learning to care about the lives of others was already a natural gift for ole Norris, and I didn't even know it. I just knew I liked cookies.

As a family, we watched Monday Night Football, where I cheered for the Pittsburgh Steelers.

As a family, we watched Monday Night Football, where I cheered for the Pittsburgh Steelers. My mom watched the Hollywood Squares and the Love Boat. Life was routine and simple.

My father was a great football player. Mel Cornell Blount played 14 seasons in the NFL He has earned many awards, owns 4 Superbowl rings and is a Hall of Fame inductee. All the while, he has always been my dad. My dad is married to a lovely woman, and I have four brothers and two sisters.

My life has been like yours, some good times, some sad. I've had many successes and many failures. I have some qualities that make me unique, and yet I am still just like you.

One day, when I was about 8 years old someone told me, "You're old enough to sign up for youth football; here's a football Norris, run!"

And the journey began. Football has been a big part of my life for many years. People look at me, and they guess I may have had something to do with sports. I have. I love football. My father, Mel Blount, loves football. He has14 seasons in the NFL, with many awards. My brothers love football, my son loves football, and most of my friends love football. The one thing I knew my whole life, was that football and sports were part of me; but I didn't know how.

One day, when I was about 8 years old someone told me, "You're old enough to sign up for youth football; here's a football Norris, run!"

Football made me a winner in many ways, and it opened my eyes to the work Jesus has me doing today, even though I no longer suit up and play on the field. The man I was off the field.... What? Who in the world was he? I learned to play football, but when I finally learned that the man I would be off the field was a son, husband, father, friend, I realized being a player might not be everything I was made to be.

The world cares about winning football games, and most players learn this at an early age. The thrill of those spoils is beyond measure. Stadiums are packed, fans wear their team colors, people go bonkers! It is a good thing to celebrate the competition, the sport, and the victors, but there is more to life than football.

Every athlete that shared a story with me while the names and places were different, the result was the same, the love of Jesus Christ.

America loves football. More than $925 million is made, just at the college level, from fans that love football. That's quite a bit of love. We love football and winners, but I am here to help you realize that the players on those teams, all of them, need to win off the field too. As part of God's team, I want to remind you that building winners, on and off the field, happens in the heart.

As a chaplain for athletes at the college level, I have talked to hundreds of athletes. Many of them came to me with head knowledge of church and Jesus, but many had never experienced the life-changing power of the Lord Jesus Christ. Many of these athletes were just waiting for ANYONE to introduce them, "Do you know the Lord, Jesus Christ died for your sins, and if you believe in him, he will draft you to that big team for all eternity?" Coach, this is your mission field.

Most of the ones who have a walking relationship with the Lord, (even though they still had real-world struggles, we all do) would tell me about the coaches, who brought them the Lord. I didn't hear stories about guys getting lectured or special treatment, or even getting a guilt trip about knowing God. Story after story was about real coaches, teachers, and leaders who influenced their lives through unconditional, continuous and unbreakable love. Every athlete that shared a story with me while the names and places were different, the result was the same, the love of Jesus Christ.

> You are God's creation too. Somehow someway, we are the same. We are all created in the image of God.

The Reverend Billy Graham said a coach could impact more lives in a year than an average person in a lifetime. Hearing this made me realize that each athlete who did not know Jesus Christ could be reached.

The world is quick to accept and honor athletes who are exceptional. Society will ignore behaviors and allow special privileges to exceptional athletes in the spirit of winning games. In the heart of a coach who cares about the player, the person off the field is just as important as the one who can win games. In the heart of a coach who cares the player who has an education to fall back on is just as important as winning games. I have been blessed to have had a few coaches and teachers who had the heart of caring.

You are God's creation too. Somehow someway, we are the same. We are all created in the image of God. Maybe I am bald and wear a cowboy hat, that's who I am. You are who you are, and all the people you know and meet, they are who they are too. Uh huh. Now we are all on the journey together. We want to be on the journey to lead as many as we can, to win. So saddle up, there are no excuses, no mistakes and no timeouts in this game. God's game isn't for one season, it's for eternal life, and He called me to get you on the team. God wants winners, and He doesn't accept excuses. When you become a part of His team, you will wake up every morning and ask yourself, "Why me God, what can I do for you today?"

THE PLAY: FULLBACK SWEEP

The sweep is a classic play that creates an open lane to run for the goal. When you open a window by letting someone know that it is no accident that they are a part of something and that God has created this opportunity, they don't always go through it right away, but they will usually look. Create a Lane.

"Yet to all who did receive him, to those who believed in his name, he gave the right to become children of God—" **John 1:12**

"For we know, brothers and sisters loved by God, that he has chosen you." **1 Thessalonians 1:4**

"But because of his great love for us, God, who is rich in mercy, made us alive with Christ even when we were dead in transgressions—it is by grace you have been saved. **Ephesians 2:4-5**

"Turn to me and be saved, all you ends of the earth; for I am God, and there is no other. **Isaiah 45:22**

CHAPTER 2
WHY DOES GOD WANT YOU?

Ask yourself, "Do I have what it takes?" The answer is, yes. You have exactly what it takes because you were made to do what God has planned. If every one of us knew today how many days we had left, how many hours and minutes, what would we do?

Ask yourself, "Do I have what it takes?" The answer is, yes. You have exactly what it takes because you were made to do what God has planned.

There was only one man who knew. His journey began a long time ago when his parents were on their way to pay taxes in Bethlehem. That boy grew up, and he formed a team. Guys who had never played on any team before. None of them knew what lay ahead. The man was Jesus; he was the only one with the game plan. Each day, the team would gather, and because of their faith in Jesus, they would listen and then faithfully do as they were told to do. It must have taken great resilience to lead that team with no chance of winning (in the world's eyes), especially knowing who had to make the final play so that all of us could win. And Jesus did. Jesus was playing in a much bigger game called eternity.

Sometimes a coach has to see the big picture. Players may be living for the here and now, with no idea what impact their choices will have on their future. Sometimes only a coach can help them see the bigger plan.

Jesus knew his journey. God spoke to him. In today's locker rooms and team meetings, practices and classrooms, coaches, trainers, officials, and leaders in every capacity have the opportunity to build God's team. You know part of the journey, and you know some of the team, the rest is up to how you let those players know. If you have what it takes, share it with your players, make it real. This part of the journey is

> In today's locker rooms and team meetings, practices and classrooms, coaches, trainers, officials, and leaders in every capacity have the opportunity to build God's team.

where you walk the walk. It's your obligation as a believer to share God's plan with your players. You have to ask the questions, and let your players know they matter to you and to God. Jesus set the tone by washing his disciples' feet. They knew they mattered. Players who know they matter will play at their highest level. They will win games.

Let's slice this pie in a different direction. Realize this: The world is going to do everything possible to make every person on this earth believe that they don't matter. As soon as kids are able to listen, they hear negative things about themselves. Advertising, movies, and the internet are constant reminders that they just don't measure up. Sports especially can tell YOUR players that they are not good enough, fast enough, cool enough, good-looking enough, rich enough or important enough to matter. God says they matter and He needs you to tell them.

> Realize this: The world is going to do everything possible to make every person on this earth believe that they don't matter.

When you feel like you don't matter, it is incredibly hard to do anything. Have you ever had to measure up to something or someone? For nine years of my life, most people didn't really notice me. Then in 1975, my dad's career in the NFL started getting quite a bit of visibility. Luckily for me, things were pretty low key until I got to junior high and high school.

The pressure started when people started hearing about my dad's success. They knew he was a champion, they loved him. Most boys want to grow up and play for the NFL, I didn't just want to, I started to feel like people expected me to.

My dad isn't just a great player on the field, he has won battles against unfair pay, dangerous play, and racism. Today, he is the CEO of a home for boys. He is a fighter and a winner and part of my journey. It may sound intimidating to some, and honestly, people are usually a little excited to know who my dad is because of the many trophies and awards the world has given him. They should be, he is a great man. I am honored, blessed and humbled to be his son. I respect and love my dad.

We come from a big family. I have eleven aunts and uncles on his side, and that's without their spouses. People are

> With his four Super Bowl rings, his awards, and his wealth, the one thing I most admire about my dad is that he is a committed believer in the Lord Jesus Christ.

often surprised to find out my dad is just an average guy. He grew up in a home without electricity or plumbing for many years, and he never forgets the blessings he has received in this world. With his four Super Bowl rings, his awards, and his wealth, the one thing I most admire about my dad is that he is a committed believer in the Lord Jesus Christ. However, he is just one believer that God has used powerfully. The best news is, God isn't done yet with my dad. He has achieved some amazing things in his life, and I see God continuing to use him in reaching lost lives.

Because my dad is one of the guys who has done it all, he made it in the NFL. Made it big. Real Big. My dad is a great example for coaches and players alike because even when his football days ended, when those games and seasons were done, regardless of wins or losses, if he wasn't on God's team, it would have all been for nothing. I am not saying his story is perfect, or even telling his journey, but the greatest team my dad plays for is God's team and he inspires people every day.

Sometimes coaches and leaders do not see how important they are to young people. A high school coach and teacher I was blessed to work with in Atlanta was not convinced at first that leading students to God was his calling. We spent time together over several months, just hanging out, having lunch, and praying for people. I'm not sure when it happened, but today this same guy takes buses full of students to FCA summer camps and helps lead weekly FCA meetings. During my time at that school, I may have known 20 students. He has been able to reach hundreds of students every day by his example of authentic compassion for them. He had been doing the same thing for a long time and then one day he realized his game changed.

For me, meeting athletes has often led me to other interactions. It happened when I met and ministered to the women's tennis team at Baylor. Sometimes the teacher becomes the student. I love to play tennis; it's therapeutic. I liked meeting with the women's team, not only because of the sport but because most of these remarkable young women have strong faith. As time passed, my wife grew to know most of them as well, and we began having times of fellowship with them in our home. One of these young ladies is Blair Shankle.

> I realized something even more special about her; Blair made other people matter.

Blair impressed me on many levels. She's an All-American athlete, All-American student great person, beautiful inside and out, but I realized something even more special about her; Blair made other people matter. As busy as she was, she felt she could always bring someone new to our home, or to Bible study. She isn't a crusader, just a nice person who has the ability to give someone else the genuine understanding that they matter. It's a beautiful thing to see. My wife has that ability, I had known it all along but didn't realize it until I saw it in Blair.

I learned so much from watching this young woman. Part of my journey is learning from others and building from the gifts that God has given to them. No matter what road Blair chooses in life, I know Jesus has an amazing plan for her full of light and leadership. One of the best things in my journey is knowing that the people I meet will reach new lives.

Through Blair, we became friends with her entire family. Maybe God thought this was a funny way of reminding me how much He is in charge of my life. Blair's dad, it turns out, is from Lubbock. He went to Monterey High School, where I went to high school. He played baseball in Lubbock and eventually played for the Red Sox for a few years before becoming a coach himself. I didn't know any of this when I met Blair, but of course, it was part of God's plan. Jimmy Shankle and his wife Terri, have become dear friends over the years.

"As a coach, a father, and businessman, I see the value is walking the walk, on and off the field. Nothing is as important as building the people from the inside when God puts you in a position of responsibility."

All of the Shankles are athletic and successful. Brent, Brooks, Blair, and Bryce have parents who believe in family. Years of coaching and four children going through the ranks of many teams, the Shankles appreciate the support and positive guidance that can keep a young person together.

Jimmy Shankle told me, "I've worked with so many players who came to me, just beat down. Sometimes from coaches, and sometimes from parents who think the yelling and cursing and put-downs get results. When all a person, athlete or not, has been told is, 'you are no good, you didn't do it right, you are a loser....' Well, pretty soon they are going to believe it. As a coach, a father, and businessman, I see the value is walking the walk, on and off the field. Nothing is as important as building the people from the inside when God puts you in a position of responsibility. Any leader who can't see fit to let their players know how much they matter, needs to hang it up."

It's not always the score that makes you a winner. You are good enough to inspire others and make a difference on and off the field.

Our Lord is a hall-of-famer too. He is our Father who art in Heaven. Our God gave His son for all of us. When we help a player or any person become a hall-of-famer in Heaven, they will win for eternity. My dad told me that.

THE PLAY: POWER RUN

The principal of this is to run up the middle, right at the defense. There is no trickery and no secrets. Coach, don't hold back. Share the gospel boldly through action and word. This is too important for ambiguity. Make sure your players know exactly what you stand for.

"What no eye has seen, what no ear has heard, and what no human mind has conceived the things God has prepared for those who love him— these are the things God has revealed to us by his Spirit. **1 Corinthians 2:9**

"Tell everyone who is discouraged, Be strong and don't be afraid! God is coming to your rescue." **Isaiah 35:4**

"Do not worry about your life, what you will eat; or about your body, what you will wear. Life is more than food, and the body more than clothes. Consider the ravens: They do not sow or reap, they have no storeroom or barn; yet God feeds them. And how much more valuable you are than birds! Who of you by worrying can add a single hour to his life? Since you cannot do this very little thing, why do you worry about the rest?" **Luke 12:22-26**

CHAPTER 3
HUMBLED & CRUMBLED

Man, they start when we're young. I bet there isn't one person who didn't have someone ask, "What do you want to be when you grow up?"

Good question, the only problem is, sometimes what we want, and what we are may not be exactly the same thing. Why does that have to lead to so much depression and unhappiness for some? What if we instead, train each other to ask, "How can you be the BEST at whatever you are, right now?" If

> "What do you want to be when you grow up?"

someone is playing sports, and we lead them down a path of being their very best that day because they are giving it their all and they are using the wings of God to guide them, imagine what they could do tomorrow.

The world likes to humble us every day, and would even like to crush and crumble us. Jesus never had to be humbled because he willing humbled himself for us. Philippians 2:6-8 "Who, being in very nature God, did not consider equality with God something to be grasped, but made himself nothing, taking the very nature of a servant being made in human likeness. And being found in appearance as a man, he humbled himself and became obedient to death even death on a cross!" God's will for him in Isaiah 53:10, "Yet it was the Lord's will to crush him and cause him to suffer." If ever there was a guy, who might have said, "Hey everyone, it's been real fun, but I'm all out of miracles here, and things are getting kinda rough with the stone throwing, and the thorny hats. I'm going on back to Heaven, and I'll catch you on the next train!" It was Jesus.

But he didn't.

God still uses us to do things we don't think we can. Things we never planned, and sometimes things we didn't expect or know we wanted. It's His plan, not ours. Are you willing to submit your will to the Father's like Jesus did?

God still uses us to do things we don't think we can. Things we never planned, and sometimes things we didn't expect or know we wanted. It's His plan, not ours.

"Let's go stomp out some ignorance." An American History teacher said this to me one day in a little school in Tyrone, Georgia named Sandy Creek High School. Brett Garvin, a teacher and coach in a school with about 1000 students.

At one point in his career he actually thought he was not successful. Brett is one of a few guys, who exchanges with me about the pitfalls of leadership today for coaches. Garvin at the time was developing a program where he wanted to train young men to be successful in life. He told me how hard his program was on kids. Garvin's #1 Rule is for players to understand that Football is a sport and does not define the person they are going to be. However when they do play for Garvin, they will be defined as part of a team and there are no exceptions. To play for Garvin, on game day members wear the same socks, the same shoes, shirt, pants everything. Players have the same haircut, NO BLING or wild anything is tolerated.

> "Let's go stomp out some ignorance." An American History teacher said this to me one day in a little school in Tyrone, Georgia named Sandy Creek High School.

Players act with dignity and respect at all times on and off the field. Garvin told me, "Norris, football will take care of itself, but we have to take care of each other." Grades are strictly enforced. Coach Garvin is known to "Hollar" when something goes wrong. He been heard to tell the players, "You did it wrong", he hollars. Then he will add, "I still love ya, but you messed it up, don't do that again!"

At every meeting, at the end of every practice, Garvin reinforces that when he is mad, it's about what happened in the play, not at the player. His players always know he has their back. One story of a player that really proved this was former student who had joined United States Marines. While his son was serving and for years after the father of the player continued to help as a volunteer at the school in any capacity needed. Garvin asked the father why he was so devoted so long after his own son had

Day in and day out, it's tough to remember that God is changing lives all around us.

long since graduated and the man told him; "Well Coach, my son has made it through 2 active tours alive, and when I asked him what helped him the most? He said dad, I would have never made it out alive if I hadn't learned how to protect my team, and be protected by my team in football." Coach Garvin said, "We may win some games, but that's winning a life."

Garvin was part of the Sandy Creek Coaching staff, they have won a few games, 107 and counting. He's helped send 8 players to the NFL, and signed 132 College Scholarships.

I reminded Garvin of his record one day when he felt like he had not made it to the top. Rankings, statistics, annual prep scores can lend themselves to bring even a power puncher like Coach Garvin down when the negativity is all around. I walked him over to the trophy case, and we stood there and I reminded him that I might have to "Stomp out some ignorance that day". I had to remind him of all the lives of the players, and their families who had sat down to supper and prayed together because he had prayed. Day in and day out, it's tough to remember that God is changing lives all around us. All he needs us to do, is to keep stomping out the ignorance and sharing the promise of Jesus Christ.

> He kept running because it made sense. It made people happy when he ran; they cheered. He thought he was doing everything right, and he was. He played ball, went to college, played more football, got married, played more football... but he was still running.

I knew a young guy who had been told his whole life, that he was going to be a super star. From a young age, a coach said, you can run fast, here's a football.... Run!. He kept running because it made sense. It made people happy when he ran; they cheered. He thought he was doing everything right, and he was. He played ball, went to college, played more football, got married, played more football...

but he was still running. Then one day, running to score touchdowns didn't make sense anymore. God had talked to that guy. That guy was me.

In 1989 I was playing for the Atlanta Falcons. This was it, the very thing I had worked for and wanted for so long, then suddenly God changed the plan. He made it very clear that I was meant to do something else. He changed the game.

THE PLAY: QB SNEAK

A quarterback takes the snap, dives ahead while the offensive line surges forward. It is usually only used in very short yardage situations. Coach sometimes you have to take charge and make things happen. God has a plan, but He still wants to use you.

"For I know the plans I have for you," declares the LORD, "plans to prosper you and not to harm you, plans to give you hope and a future." **Jeremiah 29:11**

"Brothers and sisters, think of what you were when you were called. Not many of you were wise by human standards; not many were influential; not many were of noble birth. [27] But God chose the foolish things of the world to shame the wise; God chose the weak things of the world to shame the strong. [28] God chose the lowly things of this world and the despised things—and the things that are not—to nullify the things that are, [29] so that no one may boast before him. [30] It is because of him that you are in Christ Jesus, who has become for us wisdom from God—that is, our righteousness, holiness and redemption. [31] Therefore, as it is written: "Let the one who boasts boast in the Lord." **1 Corinthians 26**

"Be on the alert, stand firm in the faith, act like men, be strong." **1 Corinthians 16:13**

CHAPTER 4
WHAT DID YOU SAY GOD?

When you are called to do what God wants, will you sacrifice?

God is talking to you. Are you ready? He isn't looking for perfect people who win every game and every season. He wants the ones willing. The coaches willing to talk to Him every day, to make the sacrifice of time to share the gospel with others. The leaders willing to spend time each day in prayer. God is talking to those people hearing him right now say, "Yes, that means you!"

> God is talking to you. Are you ready? He isn't looking for perfect people who win every game and every season. He wants the ones willing.

Will you be the person who meets someone for a coffee or a coke just to visit? Will you pray for your team every day? Will you beat the urge to put things ahead of what God whispers to your heart during prayer? This isn't my story, it's yours.

Sacrifice isn't even a word used in the same context today as it was during the days of Jesus. Today a sacrifice happens at a baseball game, or it's giving up meat once a week to improve your health. If we talk about sacrifice to people today it makes them nervous.

When I was first called to ministry, I did not know what I was doing. Every day I just pray, "Lord, lead me today to be your vessel." At that time I dipped tobacco. I loved to dip. I had my morning dip, afternoon dip, and my night-time dip. One day, The Lord said to me, "Son, if you are gonna preach you are gonna need a mouth." So I quit. No one could believe that after 10 years of dipping, I just stopped.

> When I was first called to ministry, I did not know what I was doing. Every day I just pray, "Lord, lead me today to be your vessel."

But I did. God told me to, and I did. If I couldn't use my mouth, God couldn't use me. That was kinda easy. Then he said, "Norris, Go." I was still playing football at the time, and I really thought I had made a huge sacrifice. God must have been laughing. I was beginning to see and understand that I was being led to spread the word. And then one day, my football career was over. Just like that. It was not my choice, but God had prepared me.

A Coach has the opportunity to be with players more time than many other influences in a player's life. School hours, practice, games and even travel time are all opportunities to lead by example. Will that be enough? If every player, knows the Lord by the end of your season, then yes I guess so. If not, you may have to find some other time to reach that player. There may be other sacrifices you have to make to follow God's plan. One of the scariest game changers is when God opens a door for you to go to another school or team.

During my years at Baylor University, one of the greatest guys I have ever known had to make some deep sacrifices. It's hard to understand the plan God has for us when things don't look so great or seem fair.

I have met with so many coaches who have had to face this struggle. During my years at Baylor University, one of the greatest guys I have ever known had to make some deep sacrifices. It's hard to understand the plan God has for us when things don't look so great or seem fair. There are some big game changers that can seem scary at first, and later you realize God was right there.

THE PLAY: CROSSING ROUTE

A crossing route is when the wide receiver cuts across the middle of the field. He always knows that he may be sacrificing his body for the good of the team. A crossing route more times than not ends with a WHOOOO! play. Coach, be ready to make some sacrifices for the good of God's team. Be ready to take some hits, but always remember that God has your back.

You did not choose me, but I chose you and appointed you so that you might go and bear fruit—fruit that will last—and so that whatever you ask in my name the Father will give you. **John 15:16**

God is faithful, who has called you into fellowship with his Son, Jesus Christ our Lord. **1 Corinthians 1:9**

And we know that in all things God works for the good of those who love him, who have been called according to his purpose. **Romans 8:28**

So Christ was sacrificed once to take away the sins of many; and he will appear a second time, not to bear sin, but to bring salvation to those who are waiting for him. **Hebrews 9:28**

CHAPTER 5

PLAYING FOR GOD NOT PLAYING GOD

Success can make you so important. Sometimes, you can be so successful that you know more than everybody else. The minute you let that thought in your head, you have lost. Staying in a constant state of learning, and training for God's team is the only success.

When it comes to coaching most people accept a person who is enthusiastic for their team and sport. However that same revel transitioned to love for God and it seems odd.

Anything that a person is too passionate about can seem to intimidate people. When it comes to coaching most people accept a person who is enthusiastic for their team and sport. However that same revel transitioned to love for God and it seems odd. Many people do more harm than good simply being passionate about their love for God; imposing judgment on someone else without realizing it. As leaders, our job is only to share Christ with people. It's not up to us to judge them, or tell them how to live.

What did I say? God wants us to read all the rules then just go tell people about the game. That's right. We don't have to decide who gets to play; God has the plan. Let's cover this one again because it seems to be one that people get hung up on the most. He has the plan and is in control of all things. All you have to do, if you are willing to work, is to gently tell and show people by actions not always words, that God is real and that He wants them. If you are passionate, it will show by your actions not just your words.

> God wants us to read all the rules then just go tell people about the game. That's right. We don't have to decide who gets to play; God has the plan.

In the NFL 1,696 players make the teams. In 1989, there were less than 300 billion people in the world, and I was one week away from making the big time. A chance to play for the NFL. I had already made it through the preseason, a few exhibition games, I had my number and had even been on television.

When you first make it to a pro team, you are really excited and scared. I felt like I was in a dream. It really felt like I was staying in someone's guest room. The pay is great, everything is great and maybe for me I felt like I was taking over the family business. Then came that knock on the door and the guy who says, "The coach wants to see you, and bring your playbook". Every player knows that's it. As you are walking maybe things go differently for everyone, but all I could feel was relief. Something told me, I was going to be ok. It hurt, I'm not saying it didn't hurt deeply because I didn't know how everyone else would feel. It's really weird to think about it now. I'm glad I made it, and I'm proud for every player who does. It was hard. It hurt. I had God. I knew my game had changed.

My first job after getting cut from the Atlanta Falcons was working for my dad. He has a home for boys in Pennsylvania. My father has achieved many great things in life. I love and respect him, and speak to him almost every day. I can truly say he is my hero. My dad is not my hero because he played for the NFL, or because he is a Hall of Fame member, has some Super Bowl Rings (four). He's not my hero because he came from nothing, because he helps people get their lives on track, because he has faced adversity in every flavor, or because he shares my same beautiful hair style. My dad is my hero for one reason. Because when I first became a Christian, he told me, "You gotta leave that Jesus stuff at home Norris!"

If I really wanted to bring people to the Lord, I had to go back to God again and hear what He said before I could help anyone.

My dad, and my wife, who also told me I was a "weirdo for the Lord," made me realize if I really wanted to bring people to the Lord, I had to go back to God again and hear what He said before I could help anyone. And I did. I was so fired up for the Lord that I was like the black flame coming at everyone to talk about Jesus. God didn't tell me to stop being passionate or excited about my love for Him, He just told me to read, study, learn some more about how Jesus talked to people so that I could get more people to listen. I didn't want to run people off, I wanted to bring people to the Lord, so I had to be transformed.

> God didn't tell me to stop being passionate or excited about my love for Him, He just told me to read, study, learn some more about how Jesus talked to people so that I could get more people to listen.

Soon after that, a door opened. It sounds crazy, but read the Bible, there is all kinds of stuff that will blow your mind so this is nothing. I had asked to be transferred to Lubbock, Texas. Everyone I worked with assured me that there was NO way I would get that territory. I was new to the company and Texas was prized territory, but with God the impossible becomes possible. No way at all. And then they called and said I was going to Lubbock.

The main reason I wanted to be in Lubbock, was to share Christ with my family. The first night home my little sister, Ann, accepted Jesus Christ as her Savior. Ann was baptized that year and it was one of the most glorious times of my life. Score one for the Lord.

My brother, Greg, had been in college and was struggling. It was a good time to be with my family. It seemed like God had brought me home just for them. Later that year, I had the privilege of leading Greg to the Lord just a few short months before his death. My brother and I shared many conversations about Jesus during those months. It was difficult for me to understand how he could struggle so much with the world, when I was sharing all the answers with him. It had very little to do with me. I was just a vessel.

> It was difficult for me to understand how he could struggle so much with the world, when I was sharing all the answers with him. It had very little to do with me. I was just a vessel.

little to do with me. I was just a vessel. The plan for my brother was already there and through Jesus Christ love for my brother, He used me to talk to him. Talk about a game changer. Sometimes you don't even know you are playing until all the rules are different. Greg's sudden death was tough, still is. No one knows all the answers, but I do know that He had one. My brother knew that when he died, Jesus Christ, his savior would love him and welcome him. God had brought me home to Lubbock to fulfill His purpose and timing.

THE PLAY: THE DRAW

Draw plays have two purposes. One, in long yardage passing downs, the draw play is a safe way to gain a few yards, either to get out of a third-and-long situation, or to create better field position for a punt. Two, the draw play offers a chance to get the team's best runner in an open-field situation, where the runner might be able to break a longer run.

Coach, make plans for your players that give them the opportunity to come quickly to the Lord but also drop pieces of bread in case they are slow to pick up the nourishment. You never know when God may be ready to bring someone home to heaven, so there is no time like today to share the promise of the gospel. the Lord. However, little pieces of the truth will help guide a person to the light.

Trust in the LORD with all your heart and lean not on your own understanding; in all your ways submit to him, and he will make your paths straight. **Proverbs 3: 5-6**

"Go, stand in the temple courts," he said, "and tell the people all about this new life." **Acts 5:20**

"Come to me, all you who are weary and burdened, and I will give you rest. Take my yoke upon you and learn from me, for I am gentle and humble in heart, and you will find rest for your souls. For my yoke is easy and my burden is light." **Matthew 11:28-30**

CHAPTER 6

NEVER GIVE UP, WE ARE ALL LOSERS!

Accept the opportunity to change.

Even Jesus lost something, His life. When Jesus had assembled his team, and they were traveling from town to town, he always knew His divine purpose. He knew time was short, Jesus used every moment and every opportunity to reach out to every person He encountered. When he found people of this world he could help right then, he did. Why can't we do that?

> When Jesus had assembled his team, and they were traveling from town to town, he always knew His divine purpose. He knew time was short.

We do not like to lose! Have you noticed that social media is usually about how wonderful everyone's life is going? It's difficult for us to admit when we feel like nothing is going right, or that we need to change.

God tends to help those things move along. While you are busy making plans to meet someone for lunch, you might get called to something else and BAM!, God gives you a new opportunity to do His work.

I found this out when my wife wanted to buy a new house.

"Refurbished," "redux," "faux".... These are not terms we use in sports. Why do I know these words? Well, in my journey, life took my family down a road that I will tell you is nothing short of being a blessing and a test called reality TV.

> While you are busy making plans to meet someone for lunch, you might get called to something else and BAM!, God gives you a new opportunity to do His work.

There are two extremely talented people who know how to take a run-down house and turn it into an investment. They have a TV show called "Fixer Upper," and when my wife's friend told them about my family, they contacted us to see if we wanted to participate. My wife explained to me, very simply, how it would work. She told me that they were interested in us partly because we are a bi-racial family and they wanted to recognize diversity.

This is where I am reminded that I have been hit on the head many times. I told my wife, "that is fine, but I do not want to be on the show!" Denitia calmly said, "Norris, we have to appear together in order to be bi-racial."

Chip and Joanna Gaines, the people who created this TV show are great people. They care so much about shiplap. It was an exciting experience, but really out of my comfort zone. Without going into all the details about our episode, anyone who has ever had to move or remodel a home can empathize with the added stress it can bring to a family. Now, imagine cameras recording it all. Denitia, my wife knew the outcome was going to be amazing. She was persistent, she knew the plan, and wanted to see it done. She married me for my sense of style, not my ability to knock down walls, so I admitted I was a loser and we let them do their work. In the end, our home was transformed and amazing. Don't ever think that the experiences that you have in life are happenstance. God was laughing because

Don't ever think that the experiences that you have in life are happenstance. God was laughing because after years of being the son of a hall-of-famer, gaining some recognition as a football player in my own right, and building a profitable business, this one television show about building our family home had reached thousands of people, and gave us an unexpected platform to share Christ.

after years of being the son of a hall-of-famer, gaining some recognition as a football player in my own right, and building a profitable business, this one television show about building our family home had reached thousands of people, and gave us an unexpected platform to share Christ.

Another game changer. From football legend's son to house flipper star? The number of people who have seen me in my big cowboy hat on that show is crazy cool! "Remember the episode where they find the bees?", people are always saying to each other when they figure out who we are. Of course we didn't get to speak about our faith on the show, but the opportunities after have been interesting and amazing. Be ready, be on que, and watch out for bees!

> The number of people who have seen me in my big cowboy hat on that show is crazy cool!

THE PLAY: THE SCREEN

The Screen Pass is so-called because the offense sets up a screen of blockers in front of the receiver. To do this, the pass is thrown behind the line of scrimmage. Sometimes the most amazing opportunities to witness will come from something out of your zone. If you walk the walk and speak the truth, God will use you in ways you never knew existed. Coach, sometimes the greatest opportunities come disguised. Be willing to step outside your comfort zone and take on the fixer uppers in life.

As the Father has loved me, so have I loved you. Now remain in my love. If you keep my commands, you will remain in my love, just as I have kept my Father's commands and remain in his love. I have told you this so that my joy may be in you and that your joy may be complete. [12]My command is this: Love each other as I have loved you. Greater love has no one than this: to lay down one's life for one's friends. You are my friends if you do what I command. I no longer call you servants, because a servant does not know his master's business. Instead, I have called you friends, for everything that I learned from my Father I have made known to you. You did not choose me, but I chose you and appointed you so that you might go and bear fruit—fruit that will last—and so that whatever you ask in my name the Father will give you. This is my command: Love each other. **John 15:9**

CHAPTER 7
EPIC LEGACY OR EPIC FAIL?

Tell your team the truth, pray about all things, and let your team see you work hard to achieve the goals you've set for everyone.

In our current culture, "Follow me" is probably referring to social media, but to Jesus, it still means the same thing "Follow Him." There's already enough pressure on a leader's shoulders to get things accomplished, but now it's also part of the grind to post it, tweet it and email it. Athletes today need videos, letters, and websites.

> In our current culture, "Follow me" is probably referring to social media, but to Jesus, it still means the same thing "Follow Him."

Coaches have the same pressures to get the word out and so many ways to do it. While these mass media opportunities seem to have all the easy answers, relying on them may not be the answer.

With that said, there are still only twenty-four hours in a day, so choose carefully. Young people today are spending more time isolated in front of screens and technology than they are with people. It's causing increased depression, increased narcissism, and decreased test scores. Internet technology has improved how we can send information, but no one is immune to the time traps of watching cute babies who sing and dance. God needs us to set goals, and pray for His direction in what tools we use.

Growing up I heard many stories about standing up for myself and doing the right thing in every situation. Those were founding principals that I knew my father believed in, but I learned them from coaches.

God knows the names of all His sheep, and if, in your heart you listen for His word, He will tell you. It is only difficult for those who don't want to be led. In the Bible, God gives us parables to make it easy to understand His plan.

Coaches can build teams who follow them out of fear or love. I have seen both and played for both. Growing up I heard many stories about standing up for myself and doing the right thing in every situation. Those were founding principals that I knew my father believed in, but I learned them from coaches. People always want to know what coach inspired me the most. There were a few. I can name a coach at Evans Junior High that made a huge difference in my life, Coach Hutchins. He coached football, but he was my English teacher as well. I learned in his classroom, and remember him to this day because he was a great teacher. In high school there was one coach who always had my back. He was involved in a few sports, as they often were back then, and he was NOT a saint. By today's standards, he might not have been able to do or say some of the things he did. Bob Gay, at Monterey High School, told me I could run.

There were plenty of guys faster than me, and some bigger but Coach Gay told me I was stronger and faster than they were. Day in and day out, during track and football season, Coach Gay talked to me about being strong and fast. He kept my mind on being my best. He had been a runner and played college football and ran track as well. Coach Gay had been an outstanding athlete,

> Day in and day out, during track and football season, Coach Gay talked to me about being strong and fast. He kept my mind on being my best.

and he was fearless. This came at a time when there were a lot of eyes watching me. Coach Gay knew this, and he made time for me every day. We never talked about the Lord, but he taught me what it felt like to know someone believed in me. He transferred all he knew about running to me. He only expected me to do my best, and he always knew if I had or not.

There have been many coaches who were amazing leaders in different ways, but I remember how one Coach made me feel like I could be better than even I believed I could.

Jesus used his team of disciples by teaching them, and then telling them to go and share. He knew his days were numbered. He gave them the direction and showed them the way to do the will of God. I have tried to imagine what pressure Jesus must have felt thinking, "I have to turn it all over to these guys?" Real leadership is all about transferring knowledge and trusting your team. Even when Jesus knew he had a traitor on his team, he still went on.

> Jesus used his team of disciples by teaching them, and then telling them to go and share. He knew his days were numbered. He gave them the direction and showed them the way to do the will of God.

When we build our disciples and transfer winning ways, God is happy. It's a process.

The rules of having followers are still the same, on and off the field. If you want them, you have to tell your team the truth. If you don't, God will. I pray every day for my brothers and sisters in Christ. I ask God, "Use me, God, for Your will to be done."

THE PLAY: THE GO ROUTE, THE FLY ROUTE

A *go* or *fly route* is a deep route used typically when the receiver has a speed advantage over the defensive back. In the route, the receiver will run as fast as possible to get deeper than the defensive back allowing the quarterback to throw the ball in a spot where only the receiver can get to it. Coach, go deep. Keep leading your players toward long term goals. When you build someone up every day, they begin to know you mean it. You are the real deal. Find that spot for someone downfield and then let them catch the pass!

Then Jesus said to his disciples, "Whoever wants to be my disciple must deny themselves and take up their cross and follow me. **Matthew 16:24**

Preach the word; be prepared in season and out of season; correct, rebuke and encourage—with great patience and careful instruction. **2 Timothy 4:2**

CHAPTER 8
GIVE ME PATIENCE LORD, I NEED IT RIGHT NOW!

Why don't you already do all of these things for your players? You probably know this stuff, you live it, you have heard some of it before, and chances are you know three or four lives right now that need to know they can be saved and the lives of their families can be saved by Jesus Christ. It's going to take patience. Oh, not your patience. You don't have much of that, do you? I'm talking about God's patience because He's waiting for you just like He always has because like me, you are His vessel.

It's going to take patience. Oh, not your patience. You don't have much of that, do you? I'm talking about God's patience because He's waiting for you just like He always has because like me, you are His vessel.

Let's see, eternal life with God in Heaven, and we give him what, a few years, hours, minutes of our life? Every day, the Lord waits for us patiently, to believe in Him and spread the word that He is love and real. Patience doesn't come from the world. The world will tell us to hurry, to be quick, time is money. God will tell us, wait, listen.

Why do we need patience to be winners in Christ? Sometimes things don't work out when we think they will, or as we think they will. We must always keep our eyes on the Lord when we feel anxious and let God take control of things.

"I have often struggled with patience, I often want His will, His timing, and His plan revealed immediately so I can plan ahead. Then only as He can, He spoke to me again and said, "Norris, who are you? Are you doing all you can for me?"

> Let's see, eternal life with God in Heaven, and we give him what, a few years, hours, minutes of our life? Every day, the Lord waits for us patiently, to believe in Him and spread the word that He is love and real.

There was a time that God moved me to the Midwest in -16 degree temperatures.

Anyone who knows me knows that I hate the cold. I worked hard to find another job so that I could leave and after eight months I moved my family to sunny Florida. At least I tried to move my family there. I got to Georgia only to discover the job had fallen through. We stayed in Georgia for a month wondering what to do, when my old boss called and wanted to know if I wanted my job back. I really did not have a choice, so I packed my family back up and moved back to subzero weather.

Why do we need patience to be winners in Christ? Sometimes things don't work out when we think they will, or as we think they will. We must always keep our eyes on the Lord when we feel anxious and let God take control of things.

While living in the Midwest, I had the opportunity to share Christ with hundreds of people and directly impact the lives of many of those people. God had a plan and His plan was best. I just had to be a little patient for Him to reveal it to me." It was a game changer.

When the Lord finally allowed me to move south, He had already set His plan in motion.

No, we don't have patience. We don't want patience. When things get rough, sometimes we put things of the world into our lives to absorb the void of fear we have of the unknown. We know the things we want, we pray for them, please God, I am asking you, and until we see His answer we fill the void, and God watches and waits. He has the plan.

Three years later, I had served all I could on the Board of the Fellowship of Christian Athletes, but I knew I wasn't done. I went to a guy, Randy Bruno, and told him, I want to work here. Randy looked at me and said, "Better be careful, God will use a guy like you."

God used that time, and those people to transform me. It was patience. In business I had been very successful, just like in sports, at making a plan, getting ready, being in shape and playing to win. Getting up and doing it again. It works. Now, God was using me, to broker the gospel of Jesus. I had to learn to be patient, to get to know the people, to be compassionate and empathetic to THEIR lives so that the Holy Spirit could reach them. It was a game changer, and it was authentic.

Mornings were spent sending text messages to coaches I knew in Alabama. I prayed, I studied, I made phone calls. By lunch, I might have two or three people to see, not to preach to but to talk with, to see what was on their mind. Mostly to let them know I cared. I started adding my friends, family in the mix and miracles started happening.

Most of all, I was sharing with the coaches I met, how to do EXACTLY what I was doing. Sharing my journey hoping they would do the same.

Lives change every day, I've seen it happen.

THE PLAY: THE FLEA FLICKER

A trick play to make the defense think it's a run instead of a pass. As Christians, we have to lead our lives as well as help others. Sometimes we have to juggle things to do God's work, but our commitment to our personal life, family, and job is our number one responsibility. God will work things out, give it time.

But for that very reason I was shown mercy so that in me, the worst of sinners, Christ Jesus might display his immense patience as an example for those who would believe in him and receive eternal life. **1 Timothy 1:16**

CHAPTER 9
THE AMBITION ADDICTION

Why would you think you are successful if even ONE person on your team does not know the love of Jesus? Let's say things have been OK, and looks like you might have a shot at a better position, but you know you are just starting to make a difference where you are. What are you going to do? Think that might not happen? It's going to. Maybe not exactly like that, but some how, some way, when you are actually making a difference that old snake is going to find you and say, "Oh MANNNNNNN, you can do so much better, come taste this apple!"

> Why would you think you are successful if even ONE person on your team does not know the love of Jesus?

Ambition could cost you. God knows it. That old snake knows it, and the truth is, you know it too. The best part is, when it happens at least you will know you must be doing something right.

God will always give you an option out of a sin. When ambition, or greed, or lust or anything at all gets in your life, God will ALWAYS give you a way out. Sometimes people don't understand that the only way out of a sin is forgiveness, and admitting guilt. So be clear on this one. Getting out of a sin, doesn't mean, getting out of a speeding ticket, it means asking for forgiveness and accepting the debt.

Our journeys are all the same, aren't they? At one time, I believed no one would care about me unless I played for the NFL like my dad. It was ambition that took me through those years of training and stress and anxiety. Some ambition is good, as long as the driving force is good for you. I had never known I would actually make it that far. People told me I could make it, so I did. Someone told me how to manage a business, so I did that too. God kept telling me I had another way, a way to do what HE wanted and I didn't need ambition for what the world told me I needed, money and fame, I just needed faith.

> God will always give you an option out of a sin. When ambition, or greed, or lust or anything at all gets in your life, God will ALWAYS give you a way out. Sometimes people don't understand that the only way out of a sin is forgiveness, and admitting guilt.

Ambition can cost you if it is mis-directed. The Lord is always with you, and it is sometimes important to be still, and let God speak to you softly. As a coach, you can always be that voice to your players too. Silent leadership is sometimes the most remembered. The hardest thing for me to watch is an athlete who believes only in himself. The second hardest thing is to watch an athlete who has been pushed by a parent who's ambitions are being put upon their child. In neither situation have I ever seen the end result be joyous.

When I started putting this book together, my editor said, "Norris most people think you have had a charmed life. They see all these things you've achieved and people you've met. You've had it really easy, right?"

Ambition will cost you everything. When you are with the Lord, the Lord is with you. The hardest thing for me to watch is an athlete who believes only in himself.

She was joking because she knows my story, better than me most days. But I talked about the time in my life when ambition could have cost me everything. I'm just like you, and everyone else. We get caught up thinking things are going great, but without God, it isn't. Maybe some ambition is fine, even a good thing, it's just one to keep God's careful watch over though.

I meet coaches and players every day and I can't wait until tomorrow to meet more. I am still ambitious. The winners will be every single life who wants to play for Jesus.

I know there are some who are not convinced, there are plenty who may see things a little differently than me too, I will keep doing my thing. I have a big hat to wear each day, and I don't know what God has planned for me next, but I'm ready, want to be on His team with me?

THE PLAY: UP THE MIDDLE

The ball is held and run straight into the line. Leaders get tempted all the time. Easy prey. The outcome all depends on whether you hold onto the word, and do the right thing. Don't fumble.

No temptation has overtaken you except what is common to mankind. And God is faithful; he will not let you be tempted beyond what you can bear. But when you are tempted, he will also provide a way out so that you can endure it. **1 Corinthians 10:13**

Do nothing out of selfish ambition or vain conceit. Rather, in humility value others above yourselves. **Philippians 2:3**

CHAPTER 10
HANG IN THERE

When someone tells you to hang in there, sometimes it's because you're dangling by a rope, and sometimes it's a thread. God uses us many times to speak to people who absolutely do not want to hear about Him. It's either the toughest thing you'll face or the best, kinda depends on you and how you look at things. It's not unlike how you played the game. If you were the guy that started the game on the front line, then a challenge is great, but if you were on the bench until the score was up, and you kept the team GPA high, then that's okay too. God has a job for everyone.

When someone tells you to hang in there, sometimes it's because you're dangling by a rope, and sometimes it's a thread. God uses us many times to speak to people who absolutely do not want to hear about Him. It's either the toughest thing you'll face or the best.

People respond to information differently, and while we think we know them, we may not. All we can do is what God asks us to, and that is to share His word with those He places in front of us each step of our journey. Some of them may tell us they believe and they truly do. Some of them may have doubts or even may still fall into old habits, and you can't let that rip you from the work that God has you doing. Not one life is wasted if you have had the opportunity to hear them say they accept Jesus Christ and believe he died so that they can go to heaven. Not one. God's promise to us all, no matter our journey, is that when we accept His son, He accepts us.

> Not one life is wasted if you have had the opportunity to hear them say they accept Jesus Christ and believe he died so that they can go to heaven. Not one. God's promise to us all, no matter our journey, is that when we accept His son, He accepts us.

The year that my family moved home to Lubbock, my best friend, my baby brother Greg accepted Jesus Christ as his Savior. Months later, suffering from a broken heart and deep depression, he shot himself. I don't know why so many people die this way and do not believe this was God's will. My brother wanted his pain to end, a pain he felt he could not bear. I don't think he wanted to die, he just didn't want to live in pain. We have much to learn about helping people who feel this way. Jesus knew about pain and faced his death anyway. I had been with my brother and witnessed my brother as he accepted Jesus as his Savior. Maybe my life may have been for this one purpose, if so, it is good. I was with my brother Greg when he accepted Jesus, and I know he is at peace.

THE PLAY: TAKE A KNEE

The receiver signals that they will down the ball and start the play from that yard. The Clock stops. God's plan doesn't always include the world. When they collide, things happen we can't understand. As leaders, we have to remember God will not fail, but if we have to rest or weep, or share our burden, he wants us to.

Consider it pure joy, my brothers and sisters, whenever you face trials of many kinds, because you know that the testing of your faith produces perseverance. Let perseverance finish its work so that you may be mature and complete, not lacking anything. **James 1:2-8**

A psalm of David.

The Lord is my shepherd, I lack nothing.
He makes me lie down in green pastures,
he leads me beside quiet waters,
he refreshes my soul.
He guides me along the right paths
for his name's sake.
Even though I walk
through the darkest valley,[a]
I will fear no evil,
for you are with me;
your rod and your staff,
they comfort me.

You prepare a table before me
in the presence of my enemies.
You anoint my head with oil;
my cup overflows.
6Surely your goodness and love will follow me
all the days of my life,
and I will dwell in the house of the Lord
forever. Psalm 23

CHAPTER 11
WHERE'S THE TROPHY?

Wouldn't it be great if you could give a trophy to every player, every person you ever had the chance to meet and talk to about God? Maybe a little pin, or just a sticker, that said, "I'm in!" On the God Squad!" "I B Hat'n that Satan!" Of course, you could. Someone probably does, and there's nothing wrong at all with it, no sir. Just as long as everyone understands that this season, never ends. The trophy never tarnishes, and when your soul filled with the Holy Spirit helps fill another, God's giant Megatron in Heaven goes CRA----- Z!

I love the sound of the crowds cheering. I love to cheer, especially when I played high school football, those Friday

Night Lights Cheers! I LOOOOOVVVVVED the cheers. One of my favorites, "Our team is Red Hot, our team is RED Hot, Our Team is R-E-D- RED, H-O-T-Hot!" It's much better to see in person, I promise. Each week before games, we had pep rallies, and the classes would try to compete for the spirit stick. Now, I had no idea, what a spirit stick was, but when everyone was cheering, I wanted to win that too! That's the great thing about competition, the drive to win, to achieve. to get your blood pumping, it's a healthy thing. Those cheerleaders would say, that if we win the spirit stick, we will win the game! I didn't stop to think that made no sense at all. NO, I stood up in my chair, and CHEEEERRRED LOUD! At the time, I didn't know that my brain was releasing endorphins that made me happy. All I knew was that if we won that

> I love the sound of the crowds cheering. I love to cheer, especially when I played high school football, those Friday Night Lights Cheers! I LOOOOOVVVVVED the cheers.

spirit stick, and if Norris got the ball, and I ran that ball to make touch downs, I was R-E-D- H-O-T, and when Monterey won, it seemed like everyone in Lubbock, Texas was happy too. There was a teammate, who sat next to me during pep rallies, and he didn't cheer for the spirit stick. He just barely gave it anything. He didn't get to play much, and I always thought it was because he didn't try too hard. If you are in the game, you better be there for the right reasons. Winning is in the heart.

God has His own ideas for cheers. The Bible tells us with everything we have, PRAISE THE LORD.

God tells us that our salvation is a free gift. Once we have received the gift of salvation, the Lord rewards our obedience with crowns that we can throw back at the feet of Jesus.

I played many games, and we won some, and when that season was over, it was over.

God doesn't give us a spirit stick for cheering for Jesus. He doesn't even tell us to jump up on a chair and jump around to get attention to bring people to know him. There isn't a tear out coupon in the Bible to get a free T-Shirt if you join, or free travel miles for every time you pray. You better not be expecting a plaque, a watch, a name tag, fancy lanyard or even a little bracelet.

God doesn't give us a spirit stick for cheering for Jesus. He doesn't even tell us to jump up on a chair and jump around to get attention to bring people to know him.

Nope, nada, nothing tangible. What God gives us is inside each of us. The Holy Spirit is a big picture gift. It comes with a promise of eternity. A Coach who gives a player the big picture heart of a winner is helping them win for life.

Whether someone likes it or not, God created them, and He will meet them again. If you know someone who has not accepted Jesus Christ, during their journey, God will not take them into Heaven. God has a chair for everyone. Help God fill every chair. He has given every life the opportunity to have eternal life with Him.

THE PLAY: THE HAND OFF

In the game, the QB will give the ball to an RB and let him run. The glory goes to the runner. The fans go wild when it works. As a leader, help players know there is no cheering section for doing what God wants us to do.

Each of you should give what you have decided in your heart to give, not reluctantly or under compulsion, for God loves a cheerful giver. **2 Corinthians 9:7**

He said to them, "Go into all the world and preach the gospel to all creation. **Mark 16:15**

For it is written, "As I live saith the Lord, every knee shall bow to me and every tongue shall confess to God." **Romans 14:11**

CHAPTER 12
WINNING

Whoever get's to Infinity wins!

We all begin the same, and we all end the same. How you spend your time between those breaths will make all the difference. God chose you, He wants you on his winning team. Jesus chose to humble himself and accepted God's plan of crushing Him for us. He made sacrifices for me, and for you, and now He wants you to sacrifice what you know you can to share, His word. God knows you are not perfect, He knows you have too much to do already, and He is going to open new doors and new paths to create opportunities you never saw before. You are going to have people who want to know more about God, and He wants you to be ready.

> We all begin the same, and we all end the same. How you spend your time between those breaths will make all the difference.

There is only so much time in every game, in every life and God has a purpose and plan for each and every one. When things change, opportunities are created. It's been my experience and I have seen in the lives of so many others that these game changers are when God gives you the ball and really says "Run". For me, it wasn't following in the shadow of my dad's amazing famous football career. It was learning how to be a good man, father and husband and finding the path that was right for me in ministry.

Your path is just like mine, your life just like mine. Maybe your game changer isn't out of football like mine was, but whatever it is know there is a plan for you to bring players to God's team.

We don't have a scoreboard, so we can't know how this game is really going here on earth. One day at a time, one relationship at a time, one text, one phone call, one email; that's probably all you may get. It's still worth it. Make the call, send the text. Each day I listen, and God tells me who I need to send a text to, make a call to and sometimes go visit. He will do the same for you, and we will win this game. We are on the same team. You and I are the same.

There is only so much time in every game, in every life and God has a purpose and plan for each and every one. When things change, opportunities are created.

If you need a cowboy hat, let me know! You may need patience, and you will have to tell the truth, but God wants you on His team for this season and all the seasons ahead.

There is always a game changer for every life. Being prepared by knowing Jesus Christ is the only way to be ready, for what plans God has ahead for each one of us. Giving another person this knowledge is the greatest coaching skill ever. The real winners on the field will be the ones who can continue to win in life. Make each player game changer ready, one player at a time.

> There is always a game changer for every life. Being prepared by knowing Jesus Christ is the only way to be ready, for what plans God has ahead for each one of us.

THE PLAY: MAN ON MAN

The only defensive play in my playbook, because for leaders there is no other way to know Jesus Christ than through a personal relationship with Him. Your role as a leader is simply one player's life at a time. Get to know your players, and let them know you are authentic and they matter to you. Tell them God loves them and has a place for them on His Team Forever.

And Jesus came and said to them, "All authority in heaven and on earth has been given to me. Go therefore and make disciples of all nations, baptizing them in the name of the Father and of the Son and of the Holy Spirit, teaching them to observe all that I have commanded you. And behold, I am with you always, to the end of the age." **Matthew 28:18-20**

After he had dismissed them, he went up on a mountainside by himself to pray. When evening came, he was there alone. **Matthew 14:23**

ABOUT THE AUTHOR

After a successful college football career and short stint with the NFL, Norris Blount had a life-changing experience with the Lord Jesus Christ. He realized that he was not sold out for Christ and recommitted his life to the Lord. Two years later the Lord spoke to Norris, calling him into youth ministry. He served 16 years in various ministry and pastoral roles, culminating in a role with the Fellowship of Christian Athletes and serving as Assistant Director of Sports Ministries at Baylor University.

Norris holds a B.A. in Communications from Baylor University and a Masters of Biblical Studies from Covington Theological Seminary.

Norris has built an impressive business resume with over 20 years in sales and marketing. After an accomplished career with DuPont, Norris turned his attention to staffing. As a business unit manager for Fortune 500 companies and then as an area manager in the staffing industry, Norris learned how to balance and thrive in operations and sales. His experience as an autonomous manager, vast business connections and drive led him to found Excelsior Staffing in 2007 where he serves today as the company president.

Norris and Denitia Blount have four children, Natasha, Tyler, Hannah and Levi.